The Jet Set®
On a Budget: Family Travel
A Family Vacation Under $2000

The Jet Set On A Budget: Family Travel
A Family Vacation for Under $2,000
*From the national television show **The Jet Set***
BOBBY LAURIE, NIKKI NOYA, JUAN ALBARRAN

ISBN: 978-1-716-19883-0

Printed in the United States of America.

THE jet set

Travel with us each week to destinations around the block and around the globe!

Check your local TV listings for The Jet Set or watch on our website: www.TheJetSet.tv

THE jet set en Español

¿Hablas Español? ¡Viaja con nosotros en nuestro sitio web, Roku y Amazon!
Visita: www.thejetset.tv/espanol

jsn

Love travel as much as we do? Watch JSN: The Jet Set Network online and on your smart TV's!

Visit: thejetset.tv/jsn for more information!

3

TABLE OF CONTENTS

INTRODUCTION

Taking your family on a vacation is a great way to take a break from your routine, relax and spend some quality time together. However, traveling with your family can quickly get expensive and very stressful!

The key to a successful vacation on a budget is to *make plans in advance and figure out exactly how much you can afford to spend on the trip. Then remember to always stick to your budget!*

It's possible to plan a great family vacation for $2,000 and even less. Check out the ideas in this guide for affordable, fun, and memorable family vacations.

"Travel makes one modest. You see what a tiny place you occupy in the world."
- Gustave Flaubert

CHOOSING YOUR DESTINATION

There are different factors that influence the average cost of a family vacation. *Sticking to your budget is easier if you understand what can cause the price of your vacation to go up.*

To save money and plan an affordable vacation, avoid these common destination mistakes:

- **Traveling to a popular tourist destination.** Taking a trip to Miami Beach or another high demand tourist destination will make the price of your vacation go up. Food, lodging, and even transportation to these areas are higher than in lesser-known destinations. Also, the prices in these high demand destinations fluctuate with weather. The most popular destinations are usually located in warm climates making it quite expensive when the rest of the country is experiencing colder temperatures.

- **Arriving during a major event.** Festivals, sports games, concerts, and other events draw crowds. Unless you want to attend a specific event with your family, taking a trip to a city during a yearly festival or another major event will make the cost of your vacation go up. However, a lot of lesser-known destinations have local events and festivals that don't usually draw out of town crowds but would be a perfect for a family vacation. Check our website www.TheJetSet.tv under **Destinations** to find some we've recently covered.

- **Planning to go to an urban area or the beach.** The cost of living tends to be higher in urban areas and on the seaside. Consider planning a trip to the countryside or a town that is more off the beaten track.

Traveling to one of the many national parks, visiting Washington D.C. or another city with many free activities, or choosing a more secluded vacation spot are good options.

If you want to be near a beach, consider choosing a small coastal town or a vacation spot with a lake.

"The world is a book, and those who do not travel read only a page."

- Saint Augustine

REACHING YOUR DESTINATION

1. **Flying.** Flying to your destination is definitely going to make the cost of your vacation go up. Flying might make sense if you're traveling by yourself or as a couple, but having to purchase plane tickets for an entire family is likely to cause you to go over budget.

   ‣ Flying can be more affordable if you don't mind losing the "frills" usually included in your ticket.

   ‣ Low cost airlines and in some cases "ultra low cost" airlines (such as Allegiant, Spirit and Frontier) sometimes offer promotions where you can travel as cheaply as $25 each way, per-person. However, the cost of checking a bag (and even carrying one on to the plane) usually starts around $35 a person. Flying one of these airlines and taking advantage of one of these deals would be advantageous if you were planning a one or two night trip with your family in which all travelers can fit their clothes and essentials into a backpack that can fit under the seat on a plane. That would help to avoid any baggage fees.

Aside from the low cost airlines, some offer low prices on select routes and you might be able to book airfare from one large city to another for under $100 for each ticket.

Jet Set PRO Tip | Bobby Laurie:

Use Google Flights (google.com/flights) to price out airline travel before buying your ticket. The data displayed will show you the cheapest ticket, the cheapest time to travel, the cost of a round-trip based on your dates selected, or dates you want to travel in the future and it'll also tell you what's included. Additionally, you can set "alerts" to email you when the price between two cities drops!

Jet Set PRO Tip | Juan Albarran:

When you search an airline website for fares, use two different devices. Use an Apple device and a Windows. Or an Apple and an Android. The prices ARE different!

2. Driving. The most affordable way to take your family on a vacation is to drive to your destination. Let's assume that you can spend $300 of your budget on gas for the round trip. Look at the current price of gas and at how fuel-efficient your vehicle is to figure out how far you can go on this budget. This will help you select the perfect destination.

   ‣ *Prepare your vehicle ahead of time.* It's best to spend more to get your vehicle ready for a road trip even if this means that you have to choose a closer destination. Ensure your tire pressure is checked and your oil has been recently changed.

   ‣ *Renting a vehicle makes sense if your car isn't in good shape or if you'd rather not put more miles on your own vehicle.* You can rent a vehicle in your hometown and return it to a different location of the car rental chain you selected.

   ‣ Turning the car in when you reach your destination and renting another one to drive home may save you some money. Don't forget to price this out as well as a regular round-trip!

- Remember to store the phone numbers for roadside assistance in your phone or have them on hand, *just in case!*

Jet Set PRO Tip | Nikki Noya:

Road trips take planning, and they should! Find the safest route, drive past interesting, fun and educational attractions also remember to be adventurous and open. You never know what sign along the way may pique your interest and take you down a different, better road!

3. Traveling by train. It's possible to travel by train for a very affordable price, but you'll be limited to a few destinations that can be easily reached from the nearest large city.

Jet Set PRO Tip | Bobby Laurie:

If you live near an Amtrak station, check their website rountinly for deals and discounts. They often offer two-for-one tickets or a "buy one now, get one later" deal on tickets as well. This can significantly lower the cost of your trip.

***Jet Set* PRO Tip | Nikki Noya:**

Amtrak is a trip on your way to a trip! It's a cheap and easy way to add to your getaway. The journey, the scenery and the service on the train is all a part of the experience to and from your destination.

***Jet Set* PRO Tip | Juan Albarran:**

Taking the train for your next trip adds a splash of classic travel *amid the age of modern conveniences.*

If you would rather spend money on other aspects of your trip or don't want to be too far from home for one reason or another, keep in mind that you can easily plan a fun trip to a nearby city or go on a camping trip to the nearest park or campground. Creating a staycation at home is also a fun way to getaway from the norm and enjoy with your family.

THE BEST TIME TO TRAVEL

If you have children who are too young to go to school, *you can save a lot on your family vacation by traveling during the off-season.* This is a great experience since you'll get much lower prices on accommodations and even on airfare. Popular tourist spots and landmarks shouldn't be crowded, either.

Typically, traveling is more expensive around Thanksgiving, Christmas, and the months of March, June, July, and August. Avoid traveling around national holidays if possible. Keep up with us on our website, TheJetSet.tv and our travel booking section, Jet Set Trips (http://thejetset.tv/trips) as we come out of the COVID-19 pandemic to keep track how the norms before COVID-19 appear as more people get vaccinated. It's possible what we were used to by way of busy travel months may change.

Back to the topic at hand though, some destinations, however, are more affordable in the warmer months.

For instance, there are many vacation spots in the Rockies that draw tourists for the winter skiing season. These same resorts are a lot more affordable during the summer and you'll find many other fun activities.

Many people don't realize that these skiing resorts are open during the summer! This is also a good post COVID-19 vacation idea.

As for airfare, everyone asks the question: "What's the best day to buy my ticket?" No matter what you here there's never a "best day" to buy it, but there are "good days" to travel. Generally speaking, flights are lighter on Tuesday, Wednesday and Saturday making flights on those days cheaper than the rest.

"Traveling – it leaves you speechless,
then turns you into a storyteller."
– Ibn Battuta

ACCOMMODATIONS

You can find affordable lodging for your family regardless of where you want to go. *Doing some research online and booking your stay ahead of time will help you save money.*

Use these strategies to find accommodations at the right price:

1. Take advantage of the internet. Use vacation booking sites to compare prices between different hotels or other types of accommodations. You can use filters to find lodging with specific amenities.

1. Consider renting a place to stay in a nearby city. You'll still be close to all the things you want to see, but might be able to get a lower price by not staying in a popular tourist area.

2. Learn about the neighborhood. Always do some research about the area you're interested in to ensure you're renting an accommodation in a safe neighborhood and that you'll easily have access to public transit if you need it.

3. Make reservations early. Book your accommodation ahead of time since prices tend to go up as the tourist season approaches.

There are different types of accommodations to choose from, including hotels, inns, rooms rented by owners, and even campgrounds.

The ideal accommodation depends on the kind of experience you want, your budget, and the age of your children.

Jet Set **Pro Tip | Nikki Noya:**

One of my favorite apps is HotelTonight. Great last minute rates on hotels, at a big discount! Even though the name says "tonight" you can book a room for multiple nights at a time.

Planning a *Camping* Trip

The most affordable way to go on a family vacation is to go camping.

Camping isn't ideal if you have young children, but this is the perfect way to spend some quality time with your family once your children are old enough to take part in some outdoor activities. Nearby national parks, lakes, and campgrounds could be interesting destinations.

You can easily move from one campground to another, which means you can transform your camping trip into a road trip so you can visit different parks and see the country. *You can also find campgrounds within a reasonable distance of most tourist landmarks, beaches, and major cities.*

The cost of staying at a campground is usually less than $150 for an entire week. Some campgrounds give you the possibility to rent a trailer or a mobile home, which can be a good option if you don't wish to sleep in a tent.

The downside of planning a camping trip is that you're going to need to purchase camping equipment.

This includes tents, awnings, outdoor furniture, a portable grill or another appliance you can use to cook outdoors, some shoes and clothes for your entire family, and some items you can use for outdoor activities such as hiking or fishing.

Camping gear might seem expensive when you first purchase it, but you'll be able to use this gear again for your future camping trips. Borrowing camping gear from friends or relatives can be a good option if you want to save money.

Finding an Affordable Rental

If camping isn't an option, the best place to find an affordable accommodation is to look for a vacation rental. *You can usually find less costly prices if you choose a rental that is offered directly by the owner.*

There are several websites and agencies that act as third-parties for vacation rentals. Finding the perfect rental is easier and faster if you use one of these sites, but keep in mind that the price is going to be slightly higher because a fee will go to these third parties.

Using Airbnb, Craigslist, and other sites where owners can list their rentals is a great way to find inexpensive lodging.

You can narrow down your search to rentals in a specific area, look for rentals of a certain size, or look for rentals with any amenities you like.

Follow these tips when renting a house or apartment from the owner:

- Do some research on the destination you're interested in. Put together a list of potential cities or towns where you would like to stay based on how close they are to the things you want to see.

- Ask yourself how much room you need. Your family vacation will be more pleasant if there's enough room to accommodate everyone and for your children to play.

- Consider spending a little more for additional amenities that would make your vacation more fun. For example, a rental with a pool would make for an unforgettable vacation if your children are old enough to enjoy the pool.

- Check reviews and ratings before booking a rental. Sites like AirBnB publish reviews written by their users.

- Look at photographs and videos and don't hesitate to contact the owner to get more. This is a good way to ensure the rental corresponds to your needs and to get an idea of the kind of shape it's in.

- Communicate with the owner as much as possible. Try to get to know them better by asking questions about their rental. Find out how often they maintain the rental, ask for a list of amenities, and ensure you can get in touch with them if you need to.

- Discuss important details. Ask how the owner wants to receive payment and when. Is there is a rental contract? What would happen if you weren't satisfied with the rental or if you accidentally caused damages to the rental during your stay?

__Take the time to read the rental contract before deciding to book a rental and communicate with the owner as much as possible.__

Avoid booking a rental unless you're confident that you will have a great experience and that the owner is offering a quality rental.

It's possible to find a great rental for roughly $500 a week, but the price can go up or down depending on where the rental is, the size of the accommodation, and the amenities offered.

The time of the year can also influence the cost of a rental, since a busy tourist season, a festival, or another event that attracts people to your destination could make rental costs go up.

Hotels and Bed and Breakfasts

Staying at a hotel or inn might not be an ideal option for your family vacation because these accommodations tend to be more expensive. Also, it might be difficult to find a family-friendly hotel for your destination.

Staying at a hotel makes sense when you're traveling alone or as a couple, but traveling with children means that you'll most likely want to book a suite or a couple of connected rooms.

You might also want to book a hotel room that includes a kitchenette so you can prepare meals.

Depending on your destination, a suite large enough for your family will likely cost at least $150 a night. This price will go up if you book a suite in a five star hotel or choose a hotel in an expensive tourist city.

Less expensive accommodations, such as motels, are usually less desirable because of their location or level of comfort.

Booking a bed and breakfast can often be your best option. These accommodations tend to be more affordable than hotels and it's easier to find a bed and breakfast that is family-friendly. You'll save money on food since these accommodations usually provide you with at least a free breakfast. Some of them also provide other meals, drinks, or snacks.

These tips will help you find an affordable bed and breakfast for the destination you're interested in:

Look for smaller bed and breakfasts. Smaller businesses tend to offer lower prices and it might be easier to find something available.

If you want to visit a city, look for bed and breakfasts located in nearby areas. Establishments located in less popular tourist spots should have lower prices and you'll still be able to drive to see the tourist attractions you're interested in.

Check ratings and reviews before booking a bed and breakfast. Look for an accommodation that's affordable and has received good reviews from travelers who stayed there with their family.

Ensure you'll have enough room for your family to be comfortable. Consider booking another type of accommodation if you're traveling with more than two children.

Save money by choosing a bed and breakfast with shared bathrooms. This is not as inconvenient as it sounds if you choose a fairly small bed and breakfast.

Also, consider booking a room in a bed and breakfast if you want to drive to a destination that is far away and need a place to sleep for a night. This should be a more affordable option than staying at a hotel for a night.

"To awaken alone in a strange town is one of the pleasantest sensations in the world."

– Freya Stark

OTHER EXPENSES

If reaching your destination or booking your accommodations is going to stretch your budget to the limit, look for free activities to reduce your other expenses. This way, you can still stay within your budget.

Transportation

The most affordable way to go back and forth between your accommodation, the beach, or the various tourist landmarks you want to see depends on where you are. If you decide to visit a rural area, driving there so you can use your vehicle to drive around and visit different nearby villages, lakes, and beaches is usually worth the cost savings.

If you'd rather not take your own vehicle to go on a family vacation, consider renting a car for an entire week. Weekly rates are generally less per day than daily rates. The rates you will find our website are generally 15-20% cheaper than those on larger booking sites.

If you're traveling to a large city, using the local public transit system is the most affordable option. In fact, it's smart to look for an accommodation that is conveniently located near a main public transit hub.

Most public transit systems give you the possibility to buy a week-long pass and passes for children are usually offered at a discounted price. Find out more about the public transit system of the city you plan on visiting and ensure you can easily reach the different landmarks and areas you want to see. Some cities also sell "City Passes" or all-access cards that allow you to visit all the landmarks, attractions and offer you use of the public transportation system. You can find a list of cities that offer this type of card and discounts on some of them on our website, thejetset.tv/trips

Public transit is affordable, but it's safer to take a cab if you wish to stay out late. *You can save money by using ride services like Uber or Lyft instead of a traditional taxi company.* In post-COVID times, you can save even more money if you chose to use UberPOOL and share your ride with someone else.

Food

Feeding your family during your vacation can quickly get expensive if you don't have food-making amenities at your disposal. Being able to prepare your own meals will help you stay on budget.

Look for a rental with a small kitchen or purchase a mini fridge and a camping stove if you're going on a camping trip. You may be able to stick to the same budget you use to plan meals at home, but might have to choose simpler meals because of space, time, or food storage requirements. A small battery operated fridge runs about $30-45 from a big box retailer and is also perfect for road trips!

Do some research in advance to find an affordable grocery store. Plan on going grocery shopping shortly after reaching your destination and set a budget for each trip to the grocery store.

Plan to spend a little extra so you can try some of the local specialties during your trip. You can use TripAdvisor and Yelp to see which cafes, bakeries, and restaurants are the most popular in the area you plan on visiting and can also get an idea of the price range for different establishments.

Jet Set Pro Tip | Bobby Laurie:

One of my best tips: you can find local candies, cookies, and other souvenirs cheaper at the grocery store! They don't expect tourists to shop there!

Buying some food in bulk in advance makes sense if you want to go on a camping trip and won't be near a large grocery store. Purchase snacks in advance so you don't have to stop and buy food while driving to your destination.

Activities

Take the time to make a list of the places you want to visit and the things you want to do during your vacation. There is no need to plan every day of your trip in detail, but having a list of activities and things to see as well as pricing information will help you stay busy without going over budget.

If you're going to a city with some historical landmarks, plan on visiting some of them. This should be fairly affordable and is a great way to get your children interested in history. Going for a walk in a neighborhood with historical houses is free and should be very interesting, especially if you can download an audio tour!

There are many things you can do for free regardless of where you go. Most museums have free days. You can also spend an afternoon at the beach, go hiking in the woods, or simply go for a walk to discover the city you're visiting. Some cities have free festivals and other outdoor events such as concerts or fairs.

Check Groupon and other similar sites prior to your trip. This could be a good way to find some activities at discounted prices. You could, for instance, get discounted tickets for a show, book a tour at a low price, or get a discount coupon for a local restaurant.

...EVEN MORE EXPENSES!

There are <u>always</u> some unplanned expenses during a vacation. It's a good idea to have an emergency fund in case your car breaks down during your trip (remember we told you to store your roadside assistance number!) or in case you need to find a different accommodation at the last minute.

If you're going on a camping trip, you might have to use this emergency fund to purchase additional gear you didn't think you would need. It's best to invest in quality gear in the first place so you don't have to replace anything during your trip.

Find out if your health insurance will cover you while you're out of state. You might have to take one of your children to a doctor that is outside of the network covered by your insurance and might also have to buy prescriptions. Put aside $200 in your emergency fund in case you need to cover such medical expenses.

Remember to include shopping in your budget. Buying souvenirs is fun and you'll treasure the items you bring back from your trip, so plan for these purchases in advance. You might find it easier to stick to your budget if you use cash. Simply avoid carrying more cash than your budget allows for shopping.

*"Travel is the only thing you buy
that makes you richer."*
– Anonymous

IT'S TIME TO JET SET!

It's easier to find ways to save money and stay within your budget if you do plenty of research, book your trip in advance, and plan for different types of expenses. It also helps if you follow some of our pro-tips mentioned above! Those tips are learned, tried and tested from years worth of traveling.

You may not be able to fly to Paris or Germany, or maybe even take that trip cross country for $2,000 with your family, and you for sure cannot travel to Disney World or Disneyland as the cost of entry would exceed your budget completely. However, you can still take a trip with your family to break free from the everyday reality, de-stress, relax and unwind. If you catch a great sale and pack accordingly, you don't need to limit yourself to a road trip either. Take some time to visit our website, thejetset.tv, and look for the video series in both English and Spanish where we review two of the United States' low-cost airlines, and see the total cost paid, what extra fees we encountered and what the actual comfort of those airlines are. You might be surprised!

Start looking at different destinations to find the perfect place for your family vacation. Look for a spot that is affordable, not too crowded, and that will provide you with plenty of opportunities to spend quality time together as a family.

Also, shameless plug coming, watch The Jet Set! We cover many destinations which are cheap and affordable, offer many free attractions and activities, and these places may even be just a few miles away from where you are and you may not even know it.

If you have any questions about what we covered in this guide, any suggestions on where we should visit, or maybe you want to share your own Jet Set PRO tip, we'd love to hear from you! Send us a note: inbox@thejetset.tv

ABOUT THE AUTHORS
& MORE INFORMATION

ABOUT BOBBY LAURIE
CO-HOST, THE JET SET

Bobby Laurie is the only TV travel expert with actual hands-on industry experience.

Currently Bobby Laurie serves as co-host of the nationally syndicated travel & lifestyle show "The Jet Set" and as a Traffic Anchor in Washington, D.C. for iHeartMedia and ABC7.

Laurie's background in the travel industry dates back to November 2005 when he was initially hired as a flight attendant.

After initially flying for six months for US Airways (now American Airlines) Laurie had started his move up the corporate ladder and held various positions within the industry before ultimately landing as an Analyst specializing InFlight Policies & Procedures. A year and a half later, Laurie left his post to return and joined Virgin America as one of the first 200 flight attendants under the brand started by Sir. Richard Branson.

In 2009 Bobby Laurie began his move into media and created a travel blog that was designed to collect and journal the experiences he encountered while working as a flight attendant. Because of the catchy name and his unbelievable, yet true stories, the blog became widely read among airline and industry enthusiasts. In 2010 a collection of his most popular articles and journals from his website were published into a book titled "Planely Speaking: Inflight Insight from Thirty Thousand Feet."

In 2014 Laurie produced a travel series for Discovery Network's "Destination America" titled "TAKE OFF! with The Savvy Stews" which followed Laurie and another flight attendant traveling the world and experiencing local cuisine, festivals, attractions and experiences. The show now streams on Amazon. From 2013 through 2015 Laurie served as a travel correspondent on the now cancelled national morning show "The Daily Buzz" for three years and national lifestyle show "The Better Show." Until recently, he also appeared regularly on the CNN Airport Network hosting the "Frequent Traveler" segment.

Laurie is continuously tapped to lend his opinions on the ever changing travel industry by The TODAY Show, CNN, HLN, MSNBC, ABC News, NPR, The New York Times among others.

ABOUT NIKKI NOYA
CO-HOST, THE JET SET

Exercise & Fitness have always been an integral part of Nikki Noya's life.

After watching professional volleyball player Gabrielle Reece, Nikki became inspired and decided to try the sport. By her sophomore year of high school, she had made the varsity team, been (being) quickly named Team Captain and received the Scholar Athlete Award. Under Nikki's leadership, her team ranked third in the nation. Her remarkable volleyball skills led to a full scholarship to the University of Rhode Island, where her team became the Atlantic 10 Conference Champions. With her team, Nikki traveled all over the world and upon her return she joined the AVP Next Pro Volleyball Beach Tour and played across the United States.

Through her extensive travels, she recognized how obesity, poor nutrition and lack of exercise was affecting the lives of so many around the world and across the United States. With the education and tools that she had acquired and the passion that she felt for helping others, she knew that she had to share her knowledge and give back what she had learned.

As a television expert, host for "The Jet Set," wellness coach, and personal trainer she begins her message by imparting her belief that true beauty starts from within.

She strives to empower everyone to achieve vibrancy, energy, radiance, and beautiful health through fitness, nutrition and balance. They discover the anti-aging benefits of nurturing nutrition and learn how food and movement can be their greatest beauty tools and ultimate allies.

Nikki is formally Mrs. District of Columbia 2019 and currently serves as the President of Dress for Success Miami.

ABOUT JUAN ALBARRAN
CORRESPONDENT, THE JET SET EN ESPANOL

Aviation, pleasure trips and the beauty of my country Venezuela, inspired me to show the benefits of the world through tourism.

Learning and understanding new places, new cultures, and new people allow you to grow as a person and acquiring new skills and tools help you beat and succeed at the challenges that the world presents us every day.

I was born in Merida, Venezuela, the famous city of knights, I was a student at the Illustrious University of the Andes and today I have a new home in Washington DC. I firmly believe that tourism is a way of living and building a new dynamic and cutting-edge society, through the lens of my camera and my experience in travel agencies, tour operators, and commercial airlines, I can give a small sample of what the modern world offers us.

Now I can reflect my experience in The Jet Set in Spanish.

SH⊙P
THE jet set

If you're looking for airline memorabilia, a new piece of luggage, t-shirts, Jet Set logo gear or more you can find everything (and anything!) travel related on The Jet Set Shop!

EXCLUSIVE: For purchasing this book you've earned access to 20% off your first purchase! Use Promo Code: TJSFAMILY at checkout!

TheJetSet.tv/shop